This book belongs to:

_____

to:

Judge and Mrs. Bobby Simmons
Your word is a lamp to my feet, and a light for my path.
Psalm 119:105

David and Darlene Stokes
But Jesus said, "Allow the little children, and don't forbid them to come to
me; for the Kingdom of Heaven belongs to ones like these."
Matthew 19:14

I pray your legacies touch generations to come.

God's Word Is Like...
Bonus Pages and Activity Book

Copyright 2024 by Akaya Kitchen. All rights reserved.

All Bible quotations within are from the World English Bible British Edition.

Thy Word Is Like a Garden, Lord written by Edwin Hodder (1863), public domain.

Interior template designed by Akaya Kitchen
Cover design by Akaya Kitchen

ISBN: 9780997815832

Published by Akaya Kitchen

Printed in the United States of America

God's Word Is Like...

Bonus Pages and Activity Book

Akaya Kitchen

God's Word is like delicious food.
I want to enjoy it every day.

Your words were found, and I ate them.
Your words were to me a joy and the rejoicing of my heart,
for I am called by your name, LORD, God of Armies.
Jeremiah 15:16

God's Word is like a treasure.
I keep it in a safe place.

I have hidden your word in my heart, that I might not sin against you.
Psalm 119:11

God's Word is like the rain.
It always fulfills its purposes.

For as the rain comes down and the snow from the sky, and doesn't return there, but waters the earth, and makes it grow and bud, and gives seed to the sower and bread to the eater; so is my word that goes out of my mouth: it will not return to me void, but it will accomplish that which I please, and it will prosper in the thing I sent it to do.

Isaiah 55:10-11

God's Word is like milk.
I drink it to make me strong.

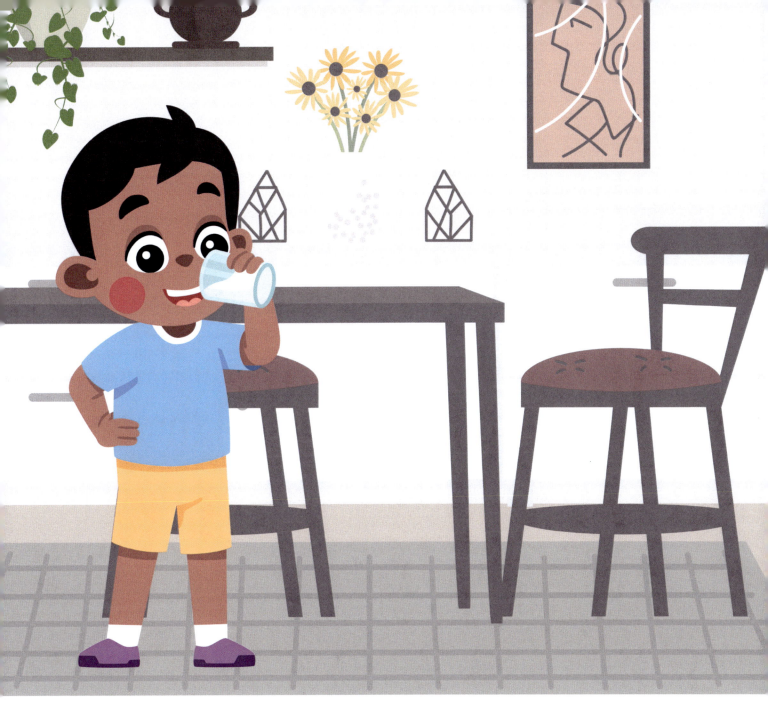

As newborn babies, long for the pure milk of the Word, that with it you may grow, if indeed you have tasted that the Lord is gracious:
1 Peter 2:2-3

God's Word is like a shield.
It protects me from bad things.

You are my hiding place and my shield.
I hope in your word.
Psalm 119:114

God's Word is like a map.
Use the map to find your way home.

God's Word is like an umbrella. Color the umbrella to give it your own design.

God's Word is like gold and silver.
Count the gold and silver trophies.

There are ___ gold trophies.

There are ___ silver trophies.

God's Word is like honey.
Find and circle all of the honey bees.
How many are there?

God's Word is like fire.
Draw lines to connect the matching
flames of fire, then color them.

God's Word is like a letter.
Write a letter back to God.

DEAR GOD,

_____

_____

_____

_____

_____

_____

_____

_____

_____

_____

_____

_____

_____

LOVE, _____

God's Word is like...
Unscramble the words to find out
what God's Word is like.

LKIM _____

RNIA _____

EIFR _____

EYHNO _____

TRWAE _____

RRROMI _____

GHU   _____

WORSD   _____

TTRELE   _____

MAHREM   _____

HSIREPW   _____

EAHCRET   _____

DSEE _____

ARBELMLU _____

PAM _____

ILTHG _____

VRIELS _____

NDCIIEEM _____

God's Word is like...
Find the words to discover what God's Word is like.

```
Q Q R S T W L R H D H W J N O
D Y F W M U O E S X A A B M E
W Z P S I R Z G T E M T R I T
X L X H R O E P R T M E I L E
H I D I N G P L A C E R A K A
J G M E D I C I N E R R W X C
X H J L S F N I S I L V E R H
S T G D M A E B N Y B L L Y E
C E O G O L D I Q Y H G E S R
W M E B A C A T X B U N R M F
P H N D Y R Z X O H O C P H O
H O J U U X M J Q H S Y F G F
```

WORD BANK:

GOLD

HAMMER

HIDING PLACE

HONEY

HUG

LETTER

LIGHT

MEDICINE

MILK

MIRROR

RAIN

SEED

SHIELD

SILVER

TEACHER

TREASURE

WATER

WHISPER

God's Word is like...
Draw a picture of what God's Word is like to you.

God's Word is like...
Solve the riddles to find out
what God's Word is like.

Riddles

I am like God's Word because I show you how you look.
What am I?

I am like God's Word because you have to listen closely to hear me.
What am I?

I am like God's Word because I keep you safe from trouble.
What am I?

I am like God's Word because I comfort you when you are sad.
What am I?

I am like God's Word because I wash you and make you clean.
What am I?

I am like God's Word because I protect you from the storms.
What am I?

I am like God's Word because I make you well when you are sick.
What am I?

I am like God's Word because I tell you what you need to know.
What am I?

God's Word is like...
Can you circle the objects that
God's Word is like?

God's Word is like...
Design your own book cover.

God's Word Is Like...

The Gospel

In the beginning, God created people in order to have a relationship with them. Sadly, people turned against God in sin, and sin separated people from Him. But God had a plan to save them from their sins.

He chose a man named Abraham to carry his promises, and God promised that He would bless all the people of the earth through Abraham's family. In the Bible, we read that God passed those promises down to Abraham's family, the Israelites, also known as the Jews. God promised that he would send an Anointed One to Israel to save the Israelites and the people of the entire world from their sins.

One day, God sent the Anointed One, His Son, Jesus (in Hebrew, His name is Yeshua), and he died for Israel's sins and for the sins of the whole world. Three days later, God raised Him from the dead, and now He is seated in heaven at the right hand of God the Father.

People from all nations everywhere are invited to put their trust in Jesus to be saved from their sins. You can also put your trust in Jesus and follow His way of living. If you put your trust in Jesus, you can say a prayer like this one:

A Prayer for Salvation

God, thank you for sending Jesus to save me from my sins. Forgive me for the things I have done wrong, and help me to live for You. Come to live in my heart and show me how to follow You. In Jesus' Name, Amen.

A Prayer for the Salvation of Israel (the Jewish People)

After Jesus rose from the dead and ascended to heaven, many Jews trusted Jesus, but sadly, most of them did not. The Bible says that one day, all of the Jews will be saved. Would you pray for the salvation of the Jewish people?

God, I pray for the Jewish people and ask
You to bring them to salvation.
In Jesus' Name, Amen.

"Brothers, my heart's desire and my prayer to God is for Israel, that they may be saved."
Romans 10:1

The God's Word...
Children's Book Series

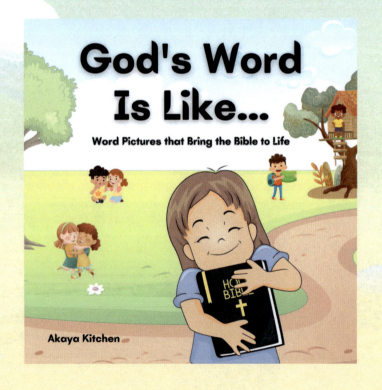

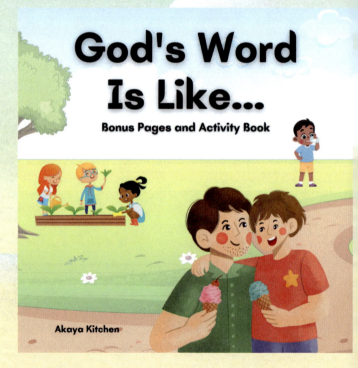

www.akayakitchen.com

For every book sold, a donation is made to Lifting up Zion.

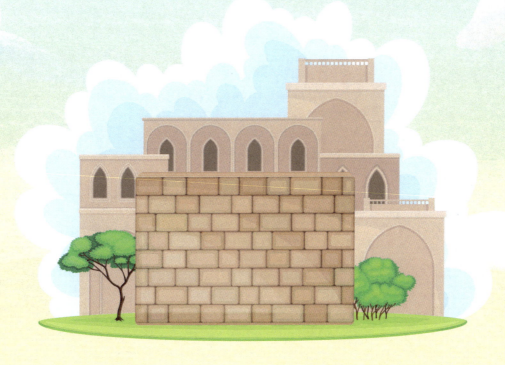

www.liftingupzion.org

Thy Word Is Like a Garden, Lord

Thy Word is like a garden, Lord,
With flowers bright and fair;
And everyone who seeks may pluck
A lovely cluster there.
Thy Word is like a deep, deep mine;
And jewels rich and rare
Are hidden in its mighty depths
For every searcher there.

Thy Word is like a starry host:
A thousand rays of light
Are seen to guide the traveler,
And make his pathway bright.
Thy Word is like an armory,
Where soldiers may repair,
And find, for life's long battle day,
All needful weapons there.

O may I love Thy precious Word,
May I explore the mine,
May I its fragrant flowers glean,
May light upon me shine.
O may I find my armor there,
Thy Word my trusty sword;
I'll learn to fight with every foe
The battle of the Lord.

- Edwin Hodder
1863
Public Domain

Made in the USA
Middletown, DE
10 September 2024

60704778R00027